Help your child succeed at school

Age 7-9
Book 3

This is my book.

My name is _____

I live in _____

I am _____ years old.

Which book?

Owl has been to the library and found 10 books.

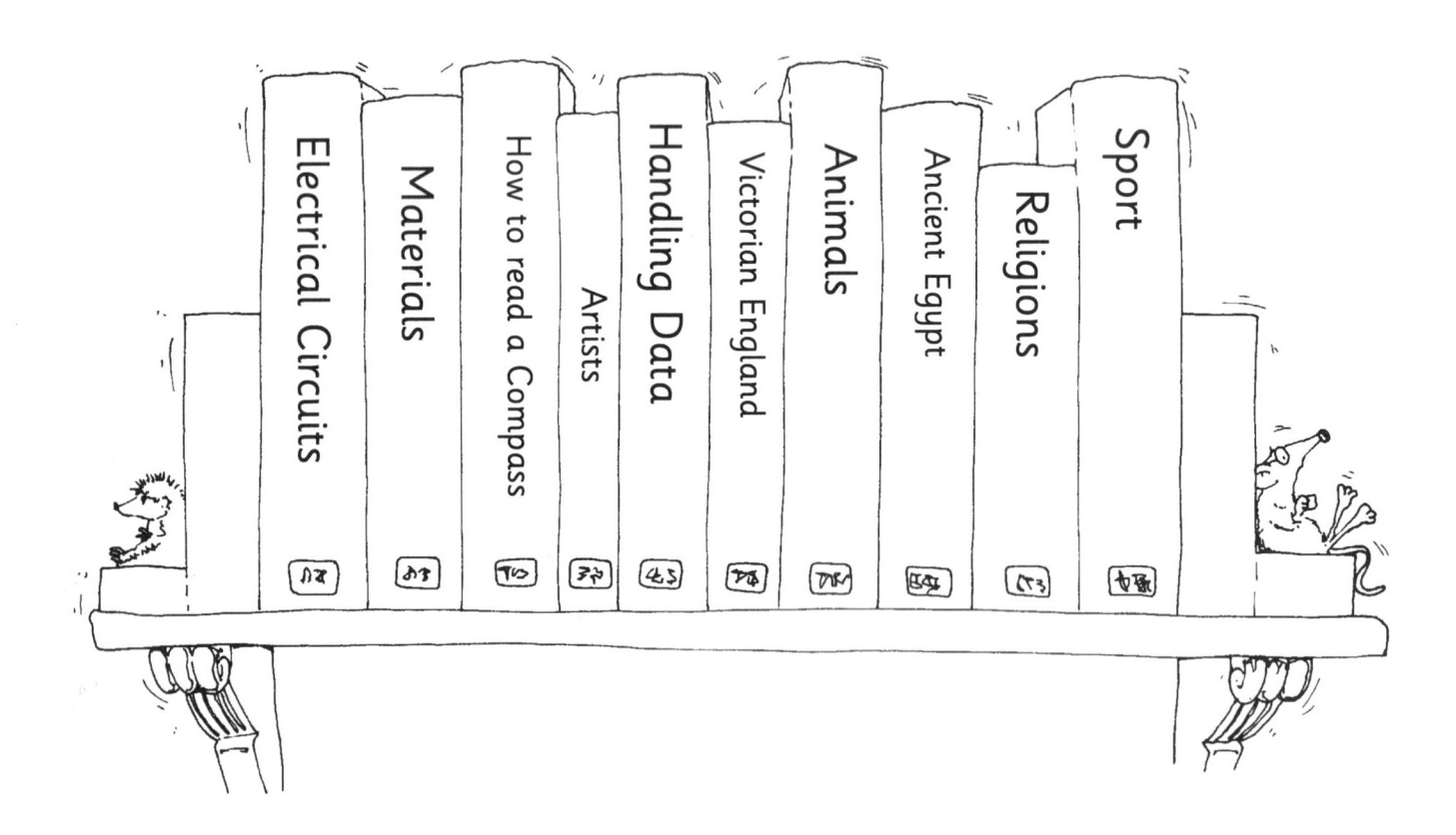

Owl needs to find out about the subjects below. Which book does he need for each one?

1. Queen Victoria _____
2. Picasso _____
3. Badminton _____
4. Cleopatra _____
5. Graphs _____
6. Electricity _____
7. Christianity _____
8. Kangaroos _____

Reading: Using reference books.

Addition

Can you do these sums?

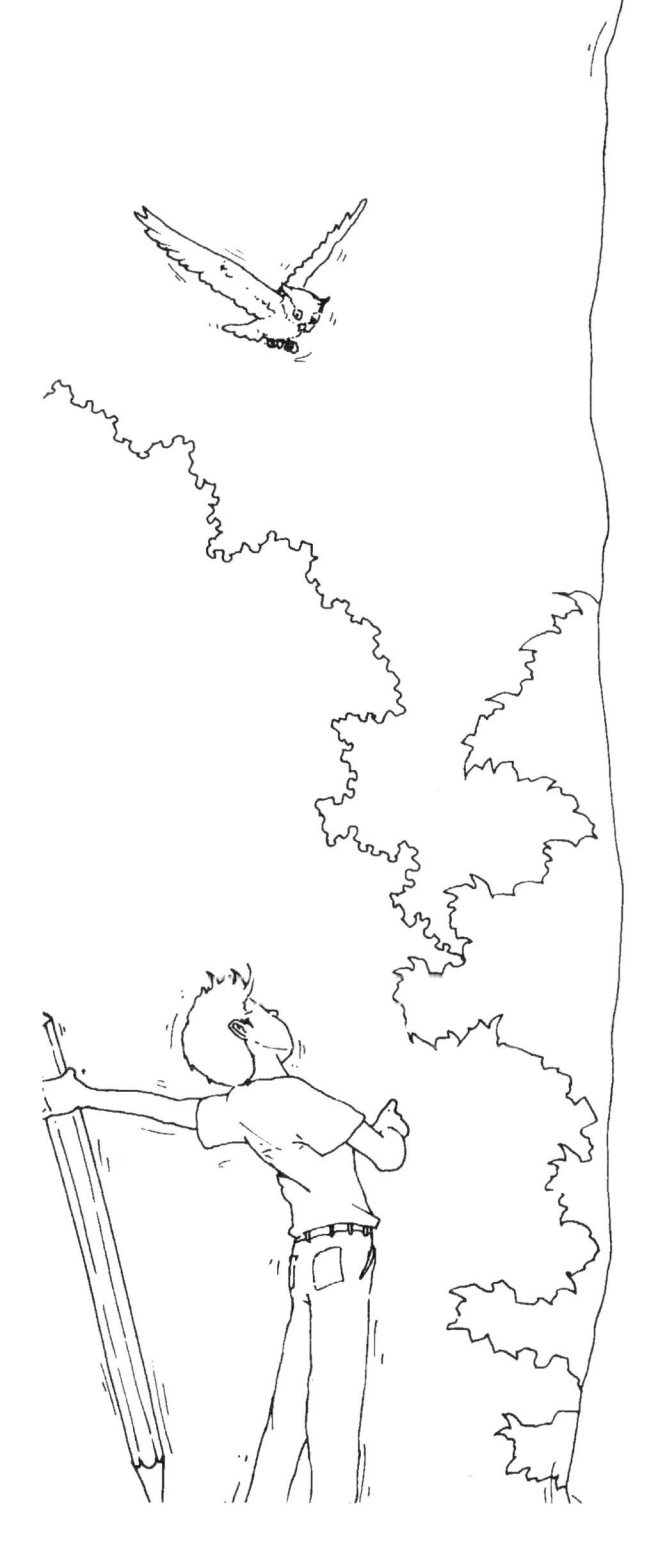

1. 670
   +216
   ___

2. 346
   +221
   ___

3. 738
   +151
   ___

4. 826
   +139
   ___

5. 675
   +206
   ___

6. 735
   +168
   ___

7. 639
   +175
   ___

8. 469
   +287
   ___

Number: Addition.

Animal habitat

The natural home of an animal is called its habitat. e.g. a goldfish lives in water. Can you match each animal to its habitat?

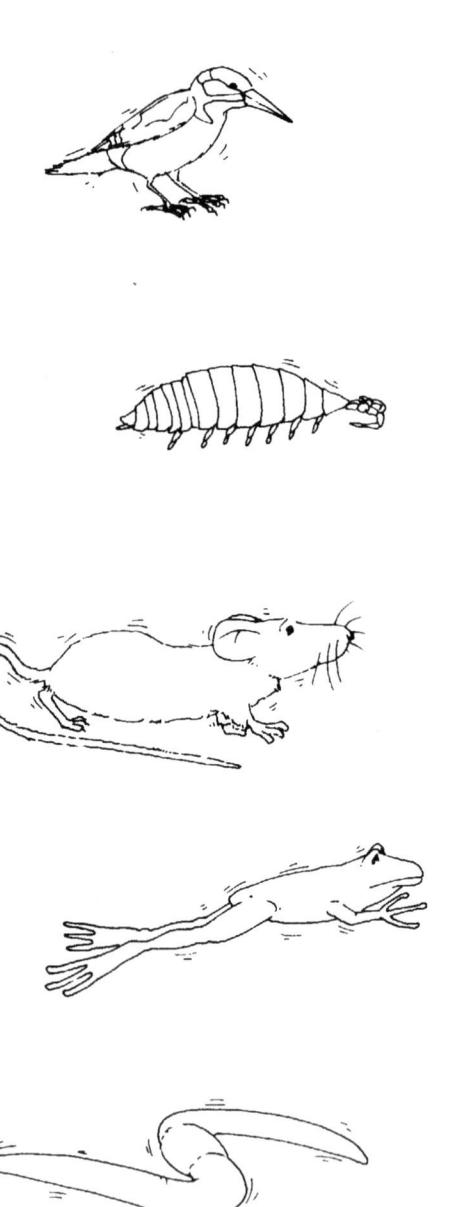

Science: Life processes and living things.

Time

We use two kinds of clock.
Here are both of them showing the same time.

11 : 45 — quarter to twelve
(eleven forty-five)

Can you put the right time on these clocks?

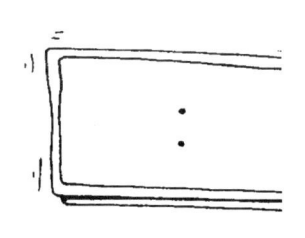

— seven o'clock

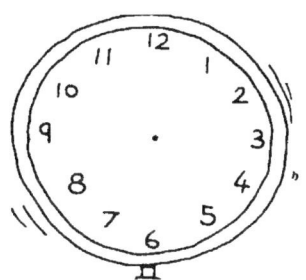

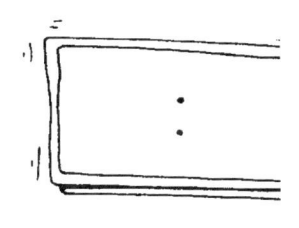

— half past eight
(eight thirty)

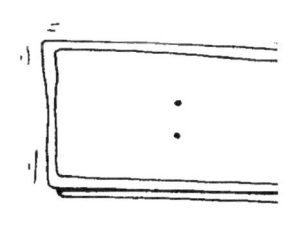

— quarter past nine
(nine fifteen)

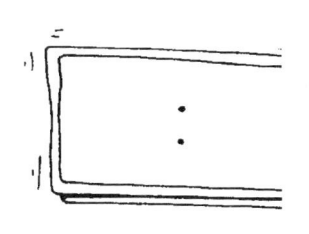

— half past ten
(ten thirty)

Shape, space and measure: Understanding time.

Three little pigs

Do you know this story?

| The wolf came down the chimney. | The wolf blew and blew the straw house down. | The wolf fell into the water. |
| The wolf blew and blew the brick house. | The wolf blew and blew the stick house down. | The three little pigs were happy. |

Put the sentences in order to tell the story.

1. _____
2. _____
3. _____
4. _____
5. _____
6. _____

English: Sequencing and re-telling traditional fairy stories.

Subtraction

Can you find out what the missing number (*) is in each sum?

Like this:

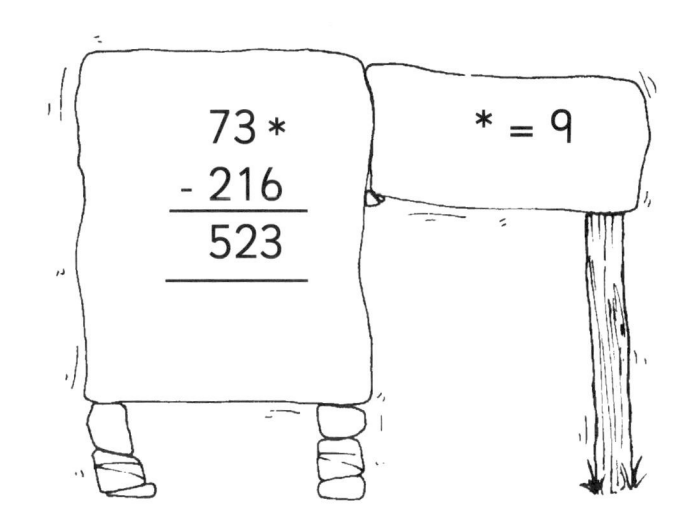

```
 73 *
- 216
-----
 523
```
* = 9
```
 739
- 216
-----
 523
```

Now try these:

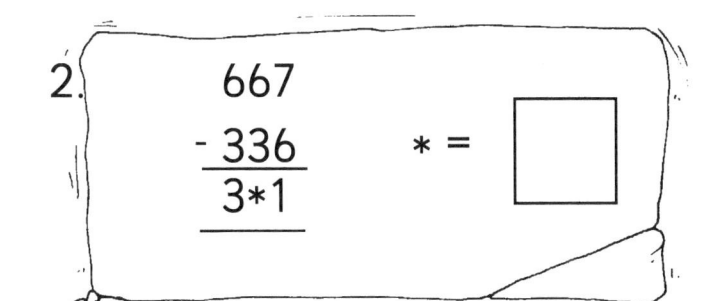

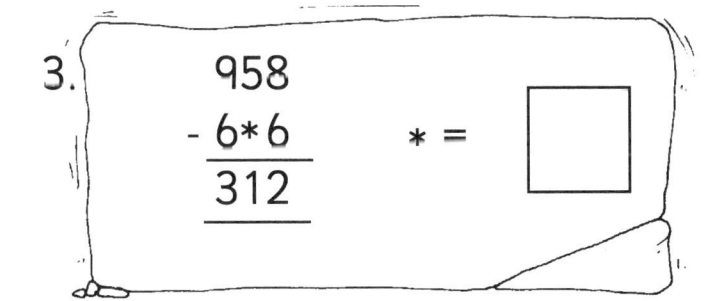

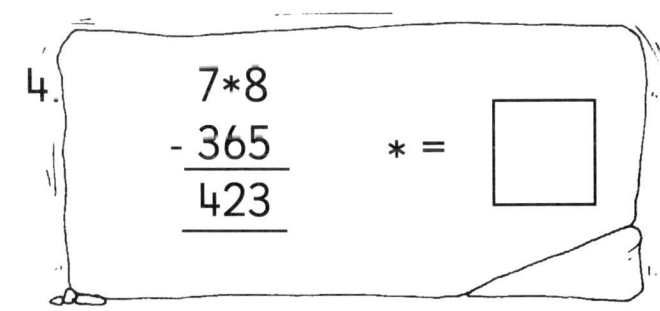

1.
```
 708
- *06
-----
 202
```
* = ☐

2.
```
 667
- 336
-----
 3*1
```
* = ☐

3.
```
 958
- 6*6
-----
 312
```
* = ☐

4.
```
 7*8
- 365
-----
 423
```
* = ☐

5.
```
 954
- 708
-----
 24*
```
* = ☐

6.
```
 372
- 168
-----
 2*4
```
* = ☐

Number: Subtraction.

Is it transparent?

Some materials are transparent (see through) and some are opaque (you can't see through them).
Can you put the materials below in the right column?

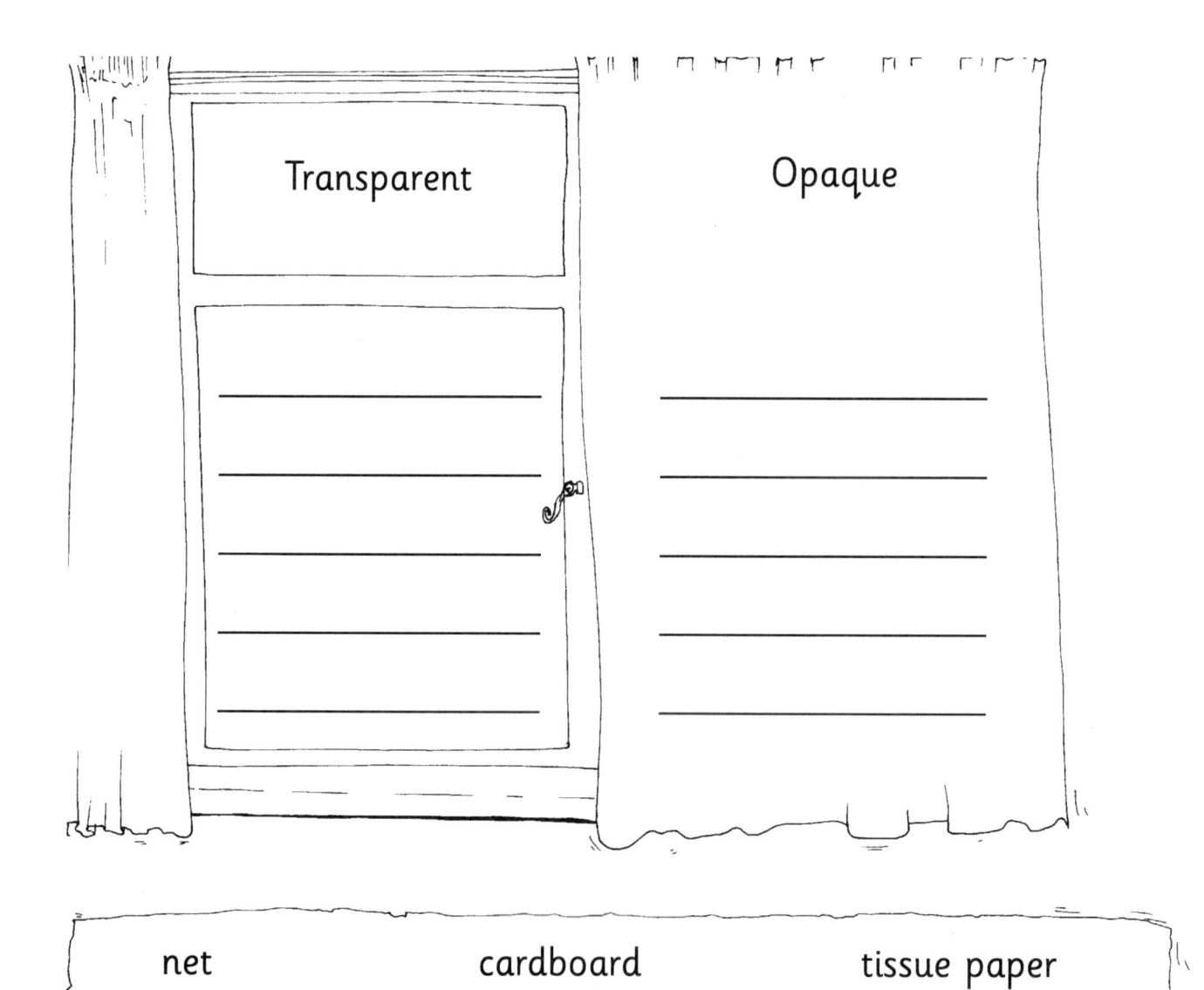

Transparent	Opaque

net   cardboard   tissue paper
cling film   light bulb   skin
window   sandpaper   fur

Science: Materials and their properties.

Beat the clock

Owl can do 15 of these sums in a minute. How many can you do?

1. 2 x 5 =
2. 1 x 2 =
3. 7 x 5 =

4. 3 x 10 =
5. 6 x 10 =
6. 5 x 5 =

7. 4 x 2 =
8. 10 x 10 =
9. 9 x 5 =

10. 3 x 5 =
11. 3 x 2 =
12. 0 x 10 =

13. 10 x 2 =
14. 7 x 10 =
15. 8 x 5 =

16. 6 x 5 =
17. 1 x 5 =
18. 6 x 2 =

19. 8 x 2 =
20. 9 x 10 =
21. 0 x 5 =

I did _____ sums in a minute.

Number: Mental recall of 2, 5, and 10 times tables.

Proper and common nouns

You already know that a noun is a naming word. There are two kinds of nouns - a proper noun and a common noun.

A proper noun is the name of a person or place e.g. London, Ian, Sam.

A common noun is the name of an object e.g. table, chair, hat.

Underline the proper nouns in red and the common nouns in blue in the list below.

house	Rachel	school	hair
London	table	England	hat
July	stone	Graham	tank
drawer	Europe	week	Monday

English: Nouns.

Area

To find the area of these shapes, we count the squares. The answer is written in centimetres squared (cm²).

Can you find the area of these shapes?

1. 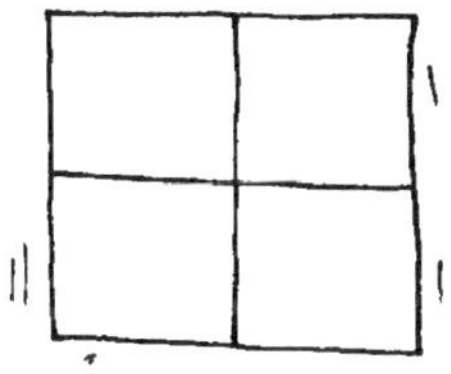 = ____ cm²

2. = ____ cm²

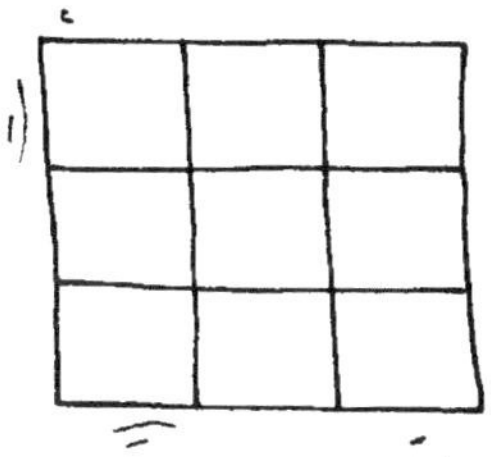

3. 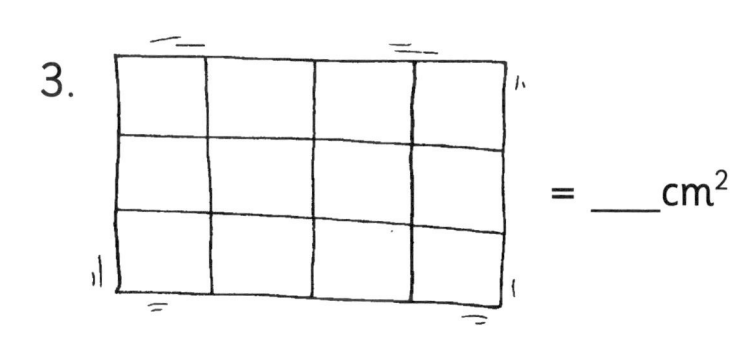 = ____ cm²

4. 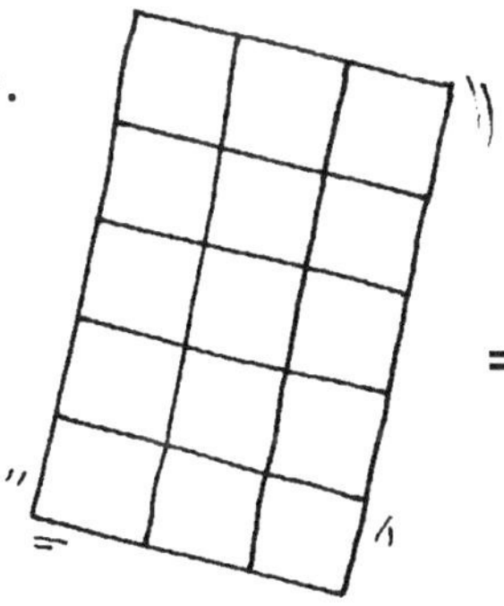 = ____ cm²

5. 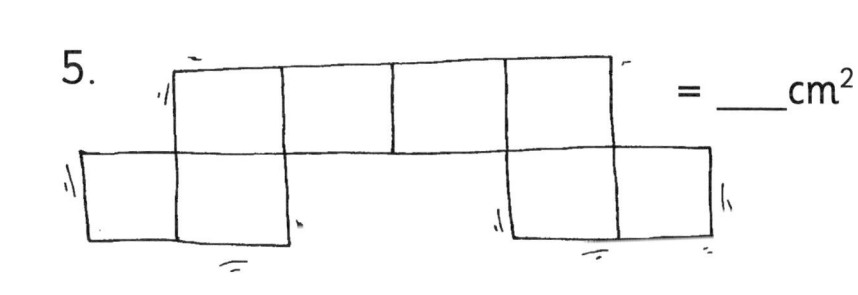 = ____ cm²

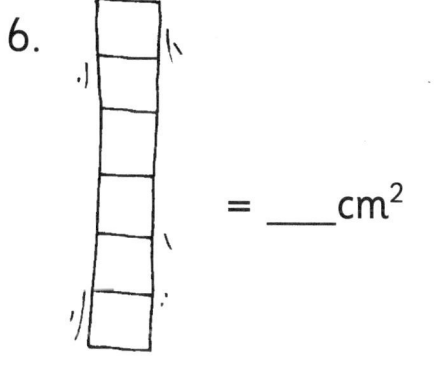

6. = ____ cm²

7. 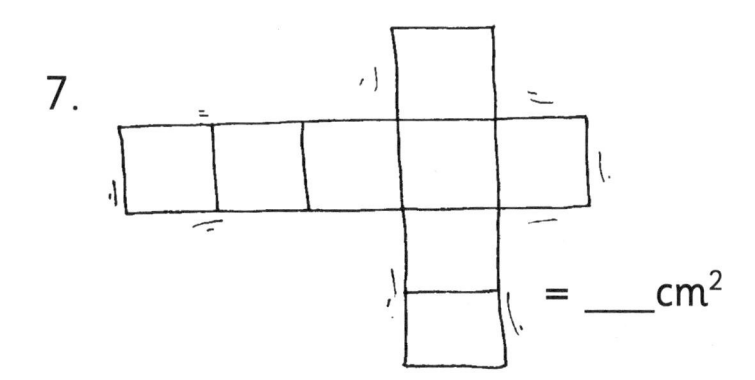 = ____ cm²

8. 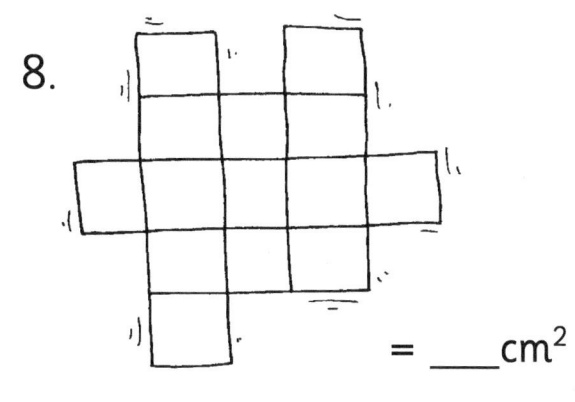 = ____ cm²

Shape, space and measure: Area.

Alphabetical order

Write the alphabet below.

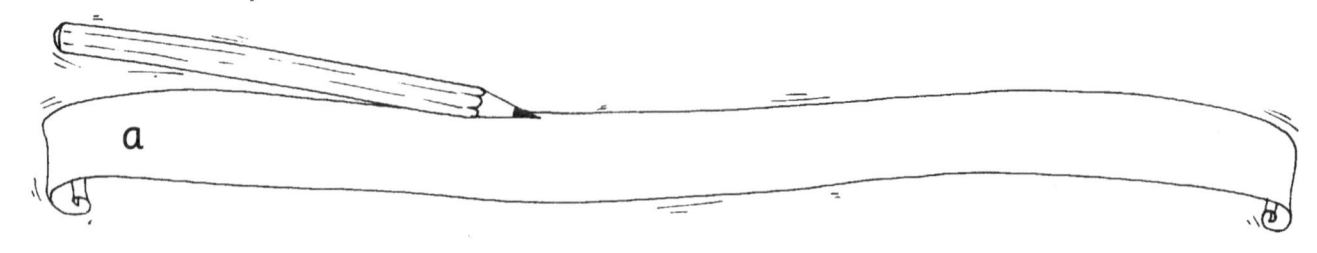

a

Now put these words in alphabetical order. The first one is done for you.

shout	shop	ship	shame
shame	ship	shop	shout

1. mask   man   match   many

2. ball   bake   battle   base

3. penny   petal   pet   pest

4. great   growl   growing   grab

English: Knowledge of alphabetical order.

Money

Ruth went shopping and bought a card at 79p, and a toy at £3.99.
She spent £4.78 altogether.

Here is the sum:

£ 3.99
£ .79
―――――
£ 4.78
 1 1

Notice how it is set out.
Now try the sums below.

1. Alex went shopping. She bought a box of chocolates for £2.79 and a pair of socks for £2.99. How much did she spend?

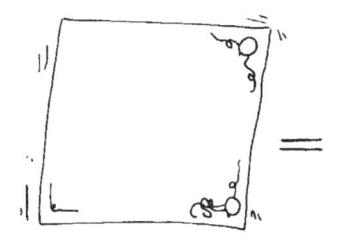

   =

2. Melanie bought a tape for £6.99 and a chocolate bar for 32p. How much did she spend?

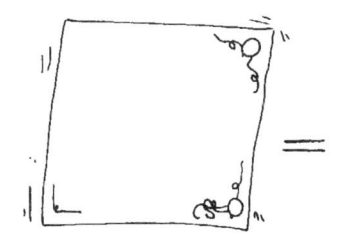

   =

3. Martin bought 2 books, a joke book for £3.49 and a history book for £3.75. How much did he spend?

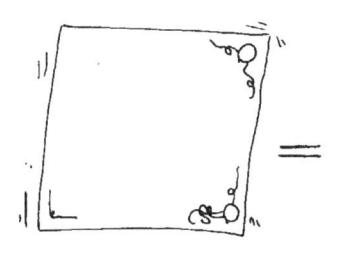

   =

Number: Understanding money.

Noun wordsearch

Can you find the nouns hidden in the square below?

w	a	t	c	h	f	a	s
q	s	a	l	d	e	d	a
l	u	p	c	e	p	b	u
d	v	i	c	m	k	e	c
x	u	n	w	s	o	d	e
m	e	b	a	c	e	v	p
f	l	o	w	e	r	z	a
t	j	o	s	a	k	g	n
b	o	k	d	n	i	k	p
p	e	n	c	i	l	l	h

book

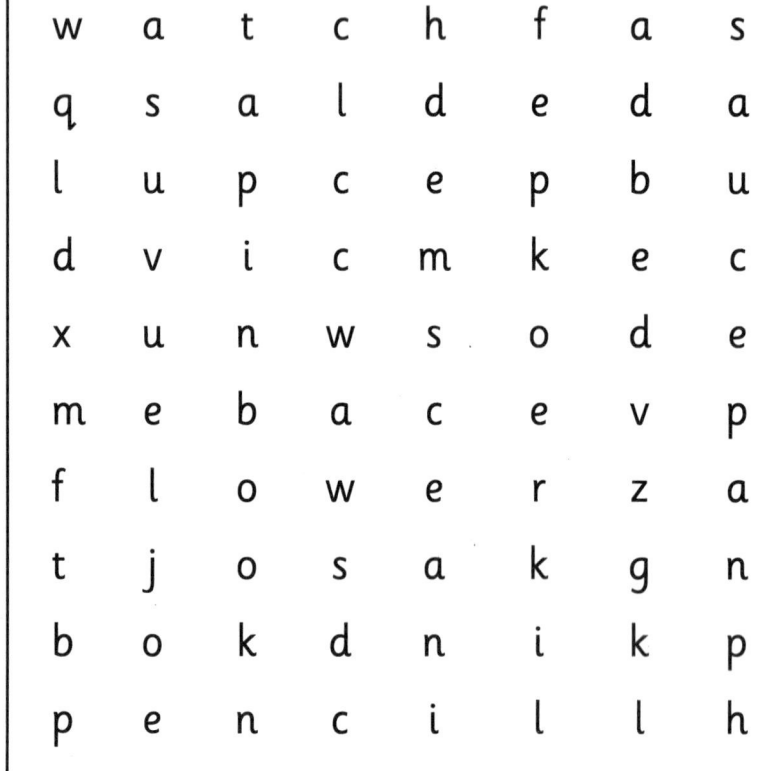

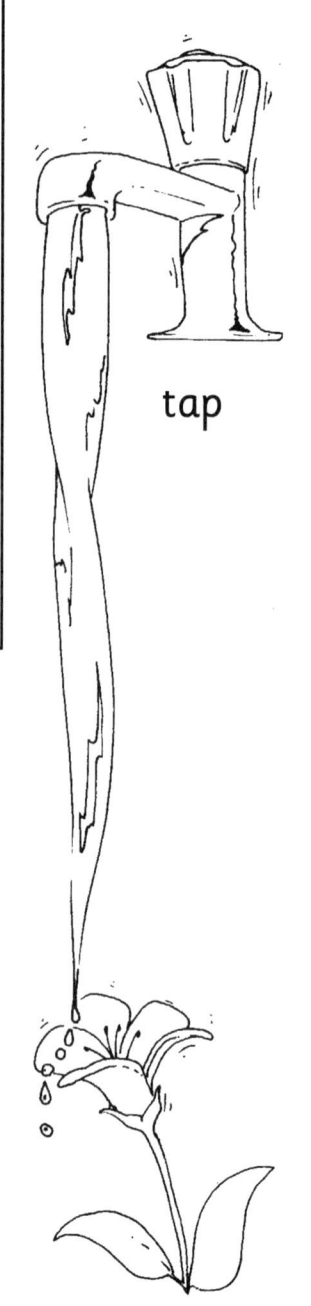

pencil

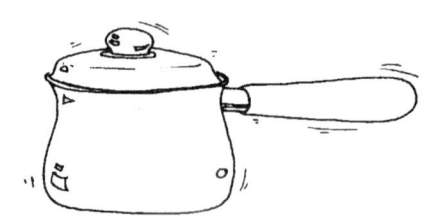

saucepan

fence

watch

tap

flower

Reading: Recognising words.

14

Digital times

Can you put the watches in the correct order? Start with the time closest to 09:00.

1.

   09 : 15   10 : 17   09 : 45

   _____   _____   _____

2. Sally started walking to school at 08:15. She arrived at Helen's house 25 minutes later. They then took 5 minutes to get to school.
   What time did Helen arrive at school?

3. Rachel caught the 10:00 bus. The journey took 40 minutes. What time did she reach her destination?

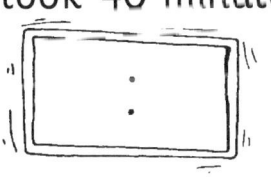

4. David left home at 06:00 to catch the 07:00 train. Unfortunately he took one hour and fifteen minutes to get to the station. How many minutes late was he?

Shape, space and measure: Understanding time.

Questions

When you ask a question you should always put a question mark at the end like this - What time is it?

Look at the questions below and re-write them, remembering the capital letter and the question mark.

when did the lesson start

_____

did Andrew win his match

_____

where did I put my school bag

_____

Below are some sentences, but not all of them are questions.
Put in the question marks where they are needed. Don't forget the full stops for the other sentences.

1. Sarah went to York on a bus
2. Did Thomas go to Spain on holiday
3. When did Samantha lose her watch
4. We have bought a new car
5. Why have you eaten all those sweets

Where are you going?

English: Using question marks.

Materials

Are these objects natural or man-made?

1.

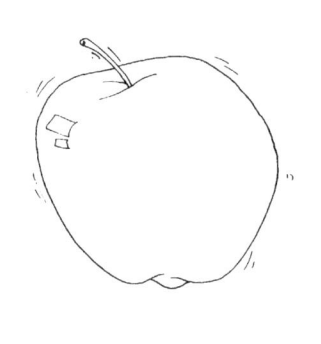

2.

3.

4.

5.

6.

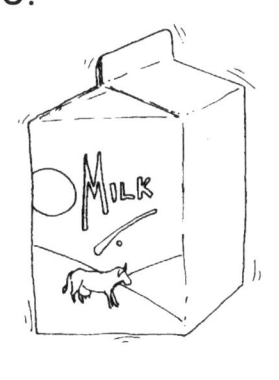

7.

8.

9.

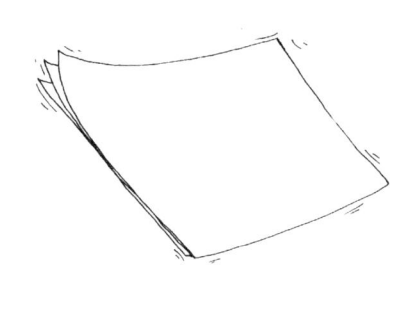

Science: Materials and their properties.

Division

Owl finds division sums difficult. He has tried these sums below. Can you check his answers? Mark them with a tick if they are correct and redo them if they are wrong.

1. 8 ÷ 4 = 2
2. 10 ÷ 5 = 3
3. 25 ÷ 5 = 7
4. 14 ÷ 2 = 8
5. 20 ÷ 2 = 10
6. 24 ÷ 2 = 13
7. 48 ÷ 2 = 14
8. 63 ÷ 3 = 21
9. 55 ÷ 5 = 12
10. 88 ÷ 2 = 43

How many did Owl get right? _____

Number: Division.

Letter writing

Learning to write a letter is very important. Below is a letter that needs completing. Imagine that you are writing to a friend you met on holiday. Remember to describe your home, friends and school.

75 Cherry Road
Bilton
Shropshire
SS24 3PD

4th September

Dear _____

_____
_____
_____
_____
_____
_____

English: Writing for a purpose.

Fractions

A fraction is part of a whole number.
This cake is split into 4 parts. When Andrew eats 1 part there are 3 parts left.
This can also be written like this: ¾

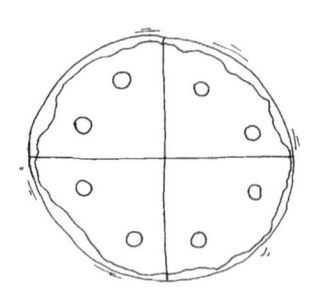

Try these! Write down how many parts are shaded.

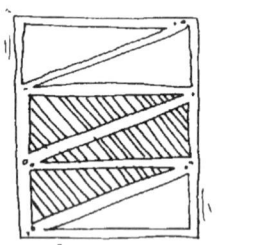

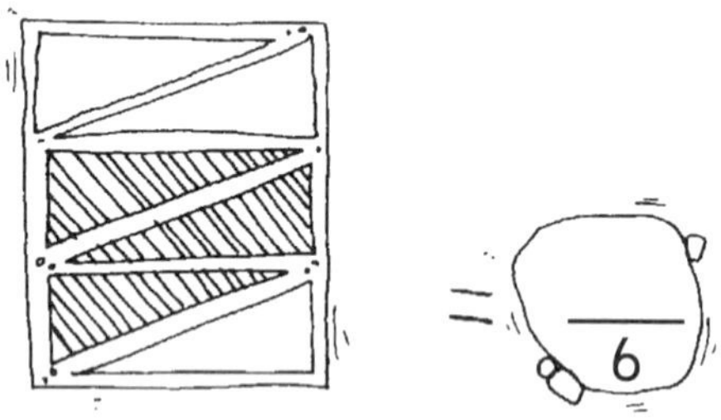

1. $\frac{}{3}$

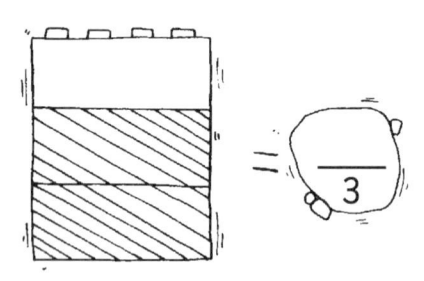

2. $\frac{}{6}$

3. $\frac{}{4}$

4. $\frac{}{4}$

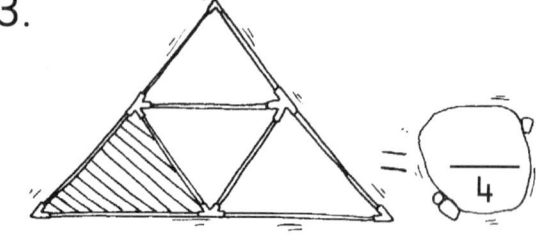

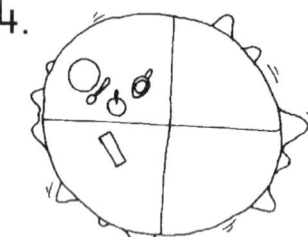

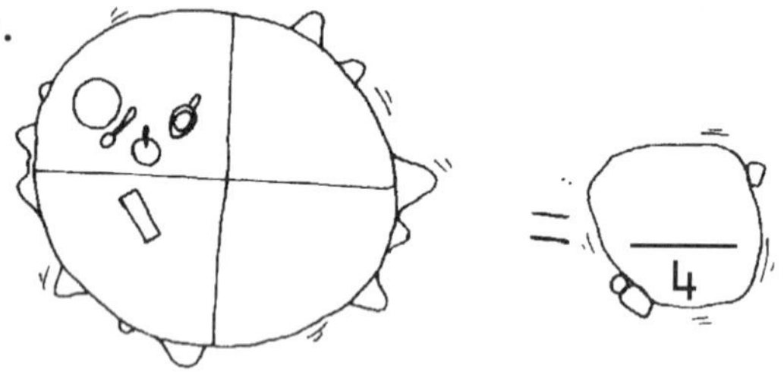

Now work out what fraction of each is **not** shaded.

5. $\frac{}{}$

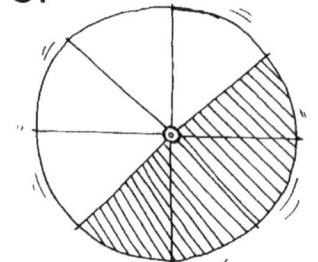

6. $\frac{}{}$

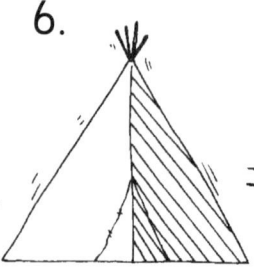

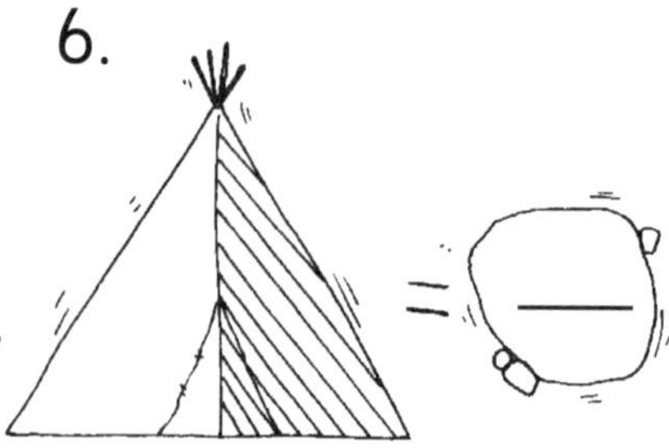

7. $\frac{}{}$

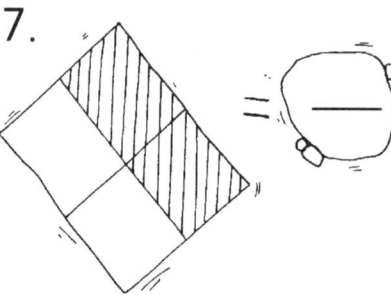

8. $\frac{}{}$

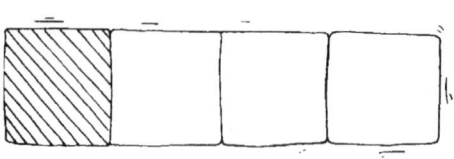

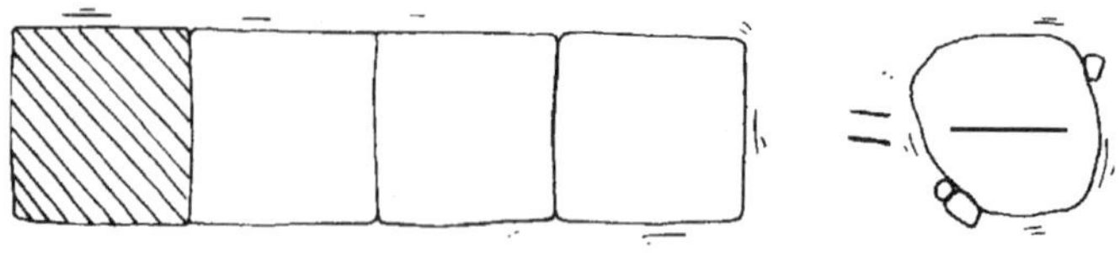

9. $\frac{}{}$

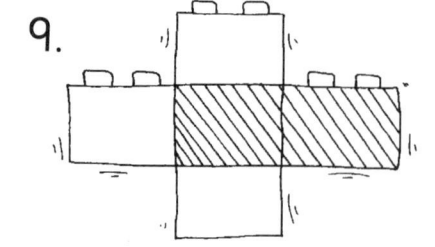

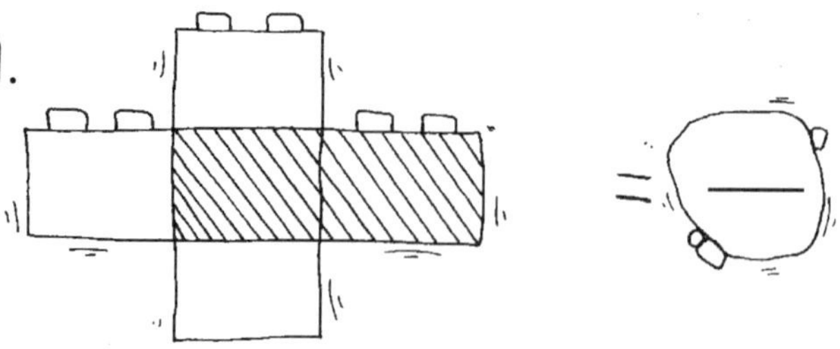

Number: Using fractions.

Similar words

Some words sound the same or almost the same, but mean something completely different.

Use a dictionary to find the meanings of these words.

to _____

two _____

too _____

Now complete these sentences using **to**, **two** or **too**.

1. You are far _____ messy.

2. I'm going _____ bed.

3. I'm going _____ London to see the Queen.

4. My Dad took me _____ the Grand Prix.

5. There are _____ ducks in that pond.

6. There are _____ many apples in that bowl.

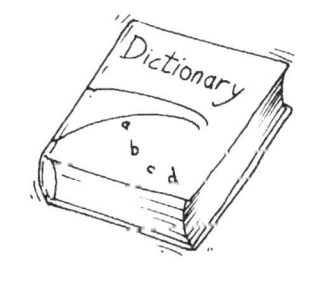

I can't carry these two bags to the car, they're too heavy!

English: Developing vocabulary.

An experiment

You will need 4 saucers and some ice cubes.

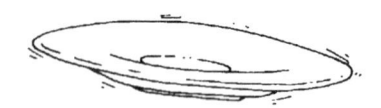

Aim: to find out what will happen to ice cubes put in different places.

List 4 places and put a tick or cross depending on whether you think the ice cubes will melt quickly there.

Place	✓ ✗

Put an ice cube on each saucer, then put the saucers in the places on your list.

What happened? _____

_____

Why do you think this happened? _____

What would happen if you returned the water to the freezer? _____

_____

Science: Experiments and investigative science.

My book

Book reviews are very useful as they tell us what a book is about. This helps people to decide whether they should read the book. Find a book that you have read recently and write a short review below.

Title:

Author:

Main characters:

Favourite character:

What the book is about:

Explain how the book made you feel when reading it:

Would you read a book by the same author again?

English: Writing for a purpose.

Electricity

Some materials conduct electricity. This means that electricity can pass through them. Metal is a good conductor of electricity, but wood is a bad conductor.

Look at these objects and put them in the correct table below.

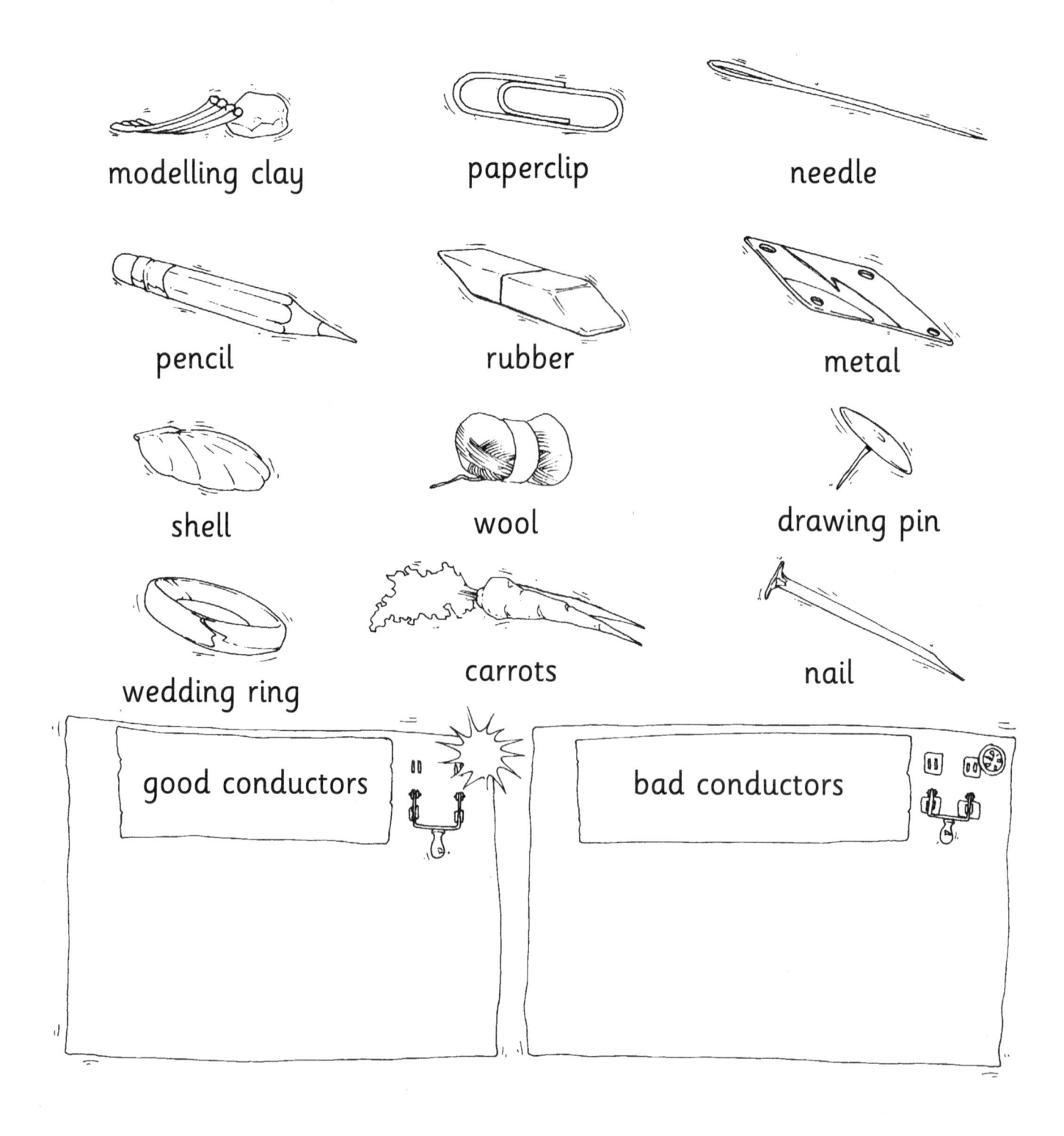

modelling clay   paperclip   needle

pencil   rubber   metal

shell   wool   drawing pin

wedding ring   carrots   nail

good conductors	bad conductors

Science: Materials and their properties.

Hidden treasure

Look at the map of Shark Island.

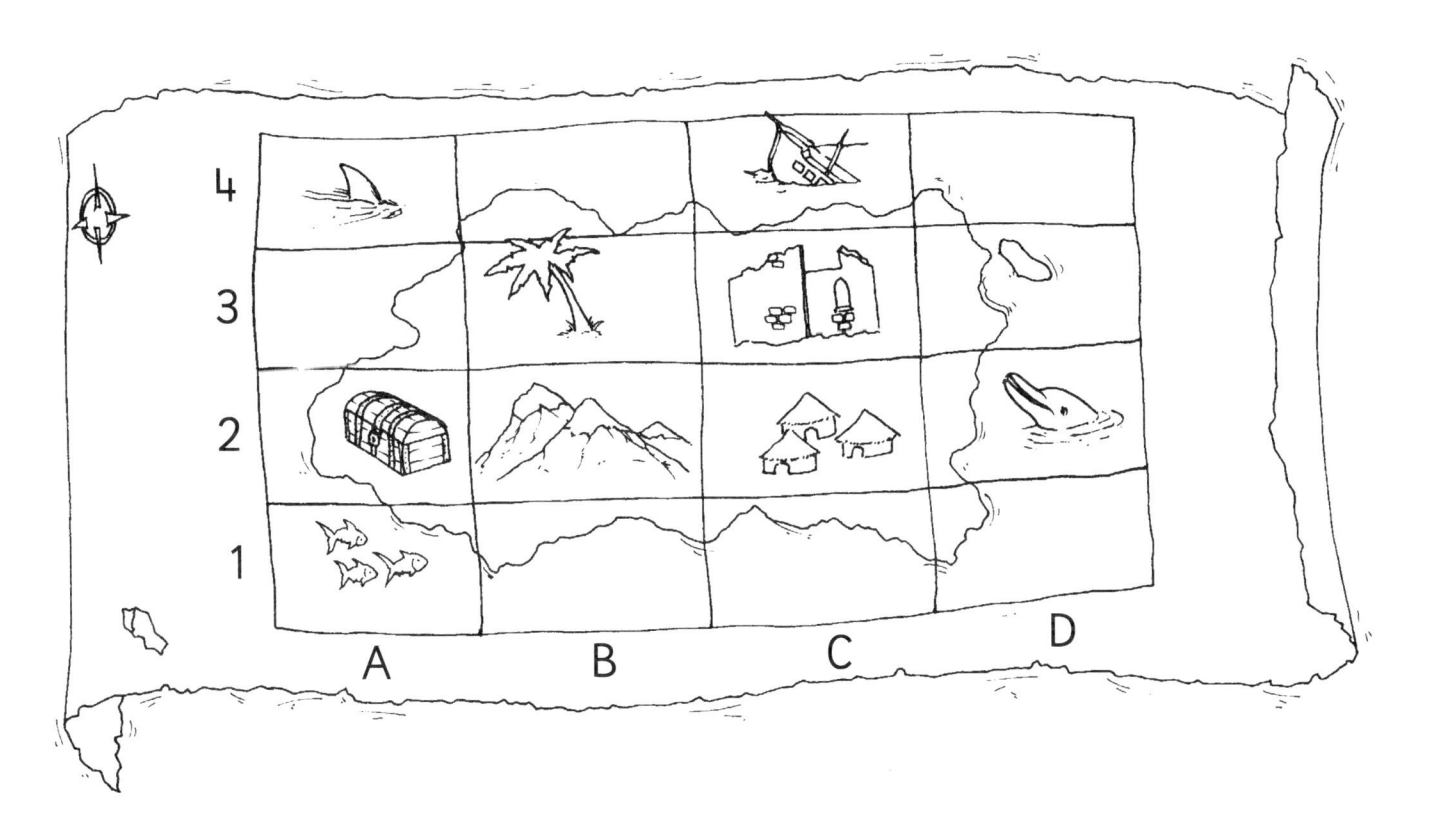

The pirates found a village at grid reference C2.

What did they find at the following grid references?

1. B2 _____
2. C4 _____
3. A1 _____
4. C3 _____
5. D2 _____
6. B3 _____

They found a treasure chest at A2. What do you think was inside?

Inside the treasure chest was _____

_____

Shape, space and measure: Understanding co-ordinates.

Crossword

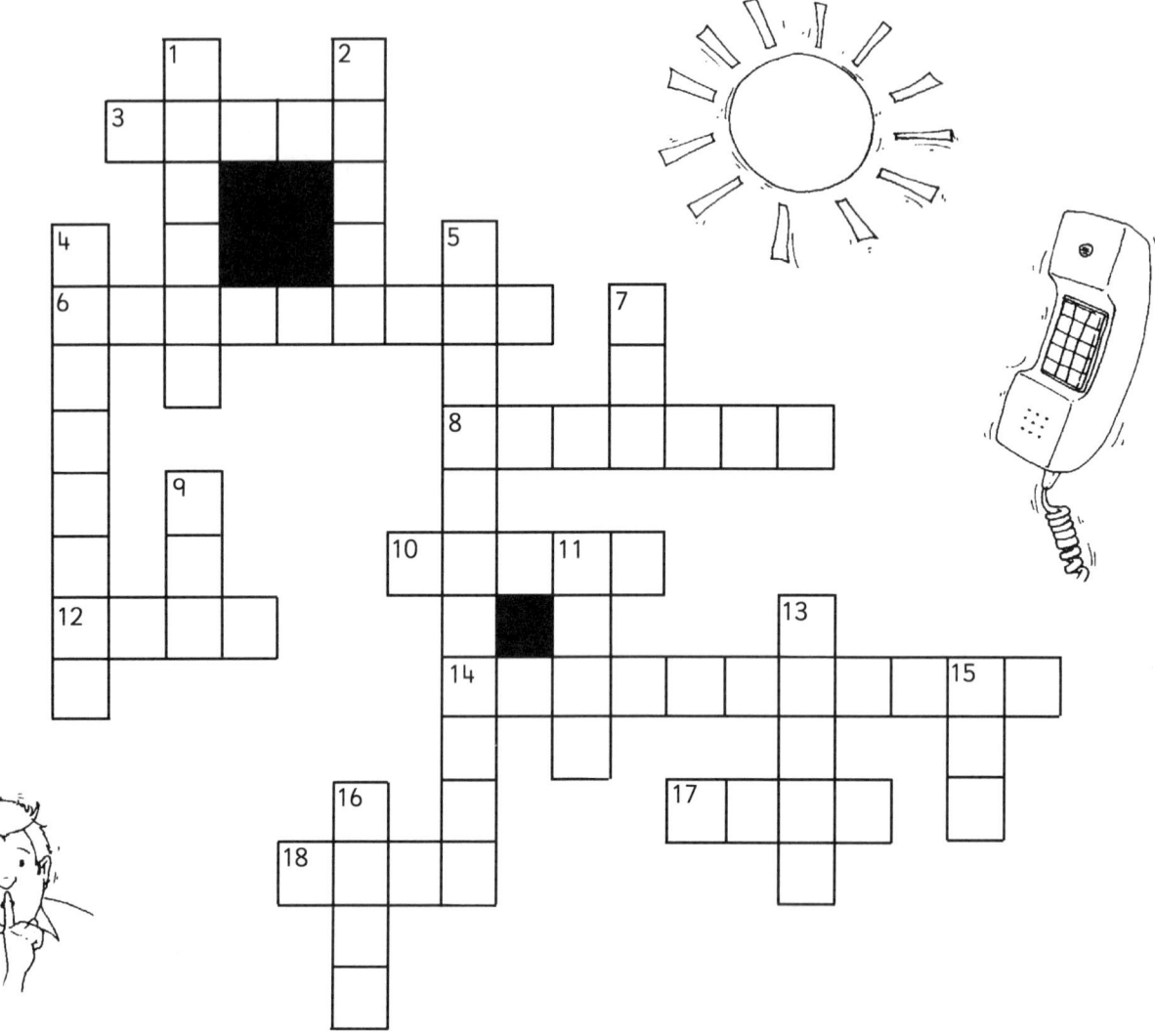

CLUES ACROSS

3. Listen to this in the car
6. Use this to talk to friends a long way away
8. The noise of lightning
10. The opposite of loud
12. An owl's call
14. What makes the lights work
17. The noise a dog makes
18. We listen with these

CLUES DOWN

1. Made of wax, often found in church
2. Hand held light with batteries
4. Light travels in a - - - - - - line
5. They make the noises in a band
7. Enables you to see in the daytime
9. The noise a cow makes
11. We use these to see
13. A cat makes this noise
15. How many ears do we have?
16. Opposite to light

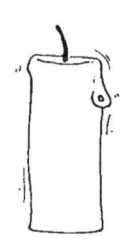

Writing: Knowledge of English language.

Speech marks

Speech marks are used to show what people have said. They go around the outside of the words people say.

Look at the words in bubbles. These are what the children are saying.

Richard: "Where are you?"
Thomas: "What are you doing?"
Samantha: "I am in the den."
Charlene: "We are having a picnic."

Write out what they said inside the speech marks.

"_____," said Richard.

"_____," said Samantha.

"_____," said Thomas.

"_____," said Charlene.

Writing: Using punctuation.

Beat the clock

How many sums can you do in a minute?

1. 43 + ☐ = 60
2. 100 ÷ 10 = ☐
3. (16 − 8) = (16 − ☐)
4. (12 + 7) = (14 + ☐)
5. 10 × 2 = ☐
6. 47 − 9 = ☐
7. 77 + 4 + 2 = ☐

8. 3 × 5 = ☐
9. 79 − ☐ = 70
10. 77 ÷ 11 = ☐
11. (2 × 3) = (3 × ☐)
12. 14 ÷ 2 = ☐
13. 63 + 3 + 19 = ☐
14. 6 × ☐ = 12

I did _____ sums in a minute.

Number: Problem solving.

Alphabetical order

Write the initial letter of each object in the boxes.

Write the words.

a _____	h _____	o _____	v _____
b _____	i _____	p _____	w _____
c _____	j _____	q _____	x _____
d _____	k _____	r _____	y _____
e _____	l _____	s _____	z _____
f _____	m _____	t _____	
g _____	n _____	u _____	

English: Knowledge of alphabetical order.

Favourite pets

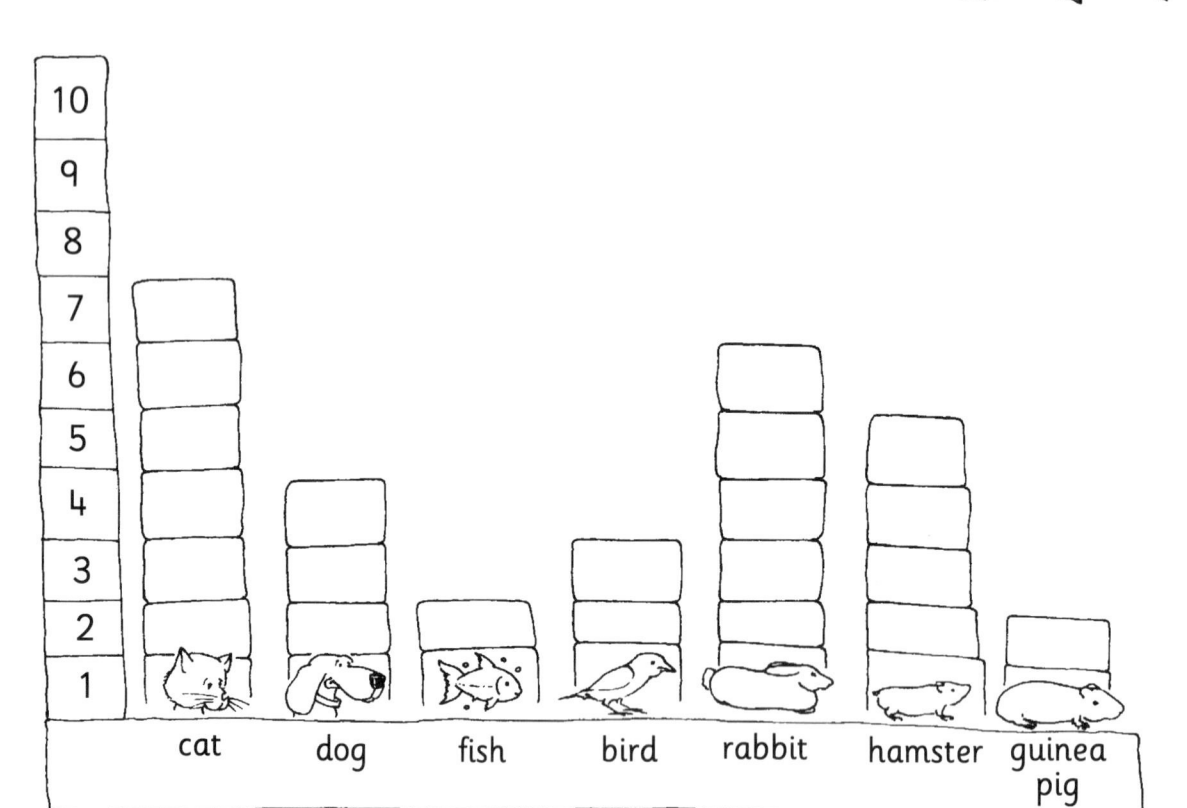

1. How many children like dogs? _____

2. Which pet is the favourite? _____

3. How many children altogether? _____

Draw the pets in order. The favourite pet is first.

Mathematics: Handling and interpreting data.

Index

We find an index at the back of a book. It helps us to find things which are in the book.

A	aardvark	p11 - 15
	ant	p 6 - 9, 15
	antelope	p32 - 36, 43
B	bear	p 6 - 8, 49
	bee	p12, 15, 26
	buffalo	p60 - 62
C	cat	p39 - 40
	cheetah	p52 - 53
D	deer	p41 - 42
	dog	p45
	donkey	p23 - 24
E	elephant	p65 - 68

1. On which pages could I find out about the following?

   ants _____   elephants _____

   cheetahs _____   dogs _____

2. If I was looking at page 61, which animal would I find out about? _____

3. What is this book about? _____

Reading: Using reference books.

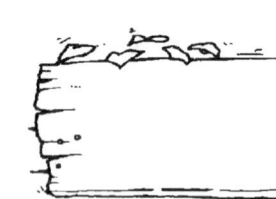

Answers

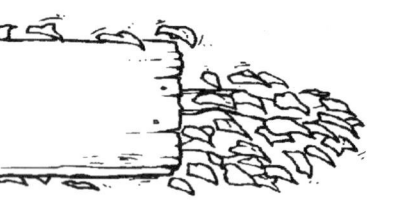

Page 2 - Which book?
1) Victorian England **2)** Artists **3)** Sport
4) Ancient Egypt **5)** Handling Data
6) Electrical Circuits **7)** Religions **8)** Animals.

Page 3 - Addition
1) 886 **2)** 567 **3)** 889 **4)** 965 **5)** 881 **6)** 903
7) 814 **8)** 756.

Page 4 - Animal habitat
woodpecker - tree trunk; woodlouse - under a damp log; mouse - straw; frog - pond; worm - soil.

Page 5 - Time
07:00; 08:30; 09:15; 10:30.

Page 6 - Three little pigs
1) The wolf blew and blew the straw house down.
2) The wolf blew and blew the stick house down.
3) The wolf blew and blew the brick house.
4) The wolf came down the chimney.
5) The wolf fell into the water.
6) The three little pigs were happy.

Page 7 - Subtraction
1) 5 **2)** 3 **3)** 4 **4)** 8 **5)** 6 **6)** 0.

Page 8 - Is it transparent?
Transparent - net, cling film, window, light bulb, tissue paper.
Opaque - cardboard, sandpaper, skin, fur.

Page 9 - Beat the clock
1) 10 **2)** 2 **3)** 35 **4)** 30 **5)** 60 **6)** 25 **7)** 8 **8)** 100
9) 45 **10)** 15 **11)** 6 **12)** 0 **13)** 20 **14)** 70 **15)** 40
16) 30 **17)** 5 **18)** 12 **19)** 16 **20)** 90 **21)** 0.

Page 10 - Proper and common nouns
Proper nouns - Rachel, London, England, July, Graham, Europe, Monday.
Common nouns - house, school, hair, table, hat, stone, tank, drawer, week.

Page 11 - Area
1) 4cm^2 **2)** 9cm^2 **3)** 12cm^2 **4)** 15cm^2 **5)** 8cm^2
6) 6cm^2 **7)** 8cm^2 **8)** 14cm^2.

Page 12 - Alphabetical order
1) man, many, mask, match **2)** bake, ball, base, battle
3) penny, pest, pet, petal **4)** grab, great, growing, growl.

Page 13 - Money
1) £5.78 **2)** £7.31 **3)** £7.24.

Page 15 - Digital time
1) 09:15, 09:45, 10:17 **2)** 08:45 **3)** 10:40 **4)** 15.

Page 16 - Questions
1) . **2)** ? **3)** ? **4)** . **5)** ?

Page 17 - Materials
Natural - 1, 3, 5, 6, 7.
Man-made - 2, 4, 8, 9.

Page 18 - Division
Owl got three right - 1, 5, 8.
2) 2 **3)** 5 **4)** 7 **6)** 12 **7)** 24 **9)** 11 **10)** 44.

Page 20 - Fractions
1) 2/3 **2)** 3/6 **3)** 1/4 **4)** 0/4 **5)** 4/8 **6)** 2/4 **7)** 2/4
8) 3/4 **9)** 3/5.

Page 21 - Similar words
1) too **2)** to **3)** to **4)** to **5)** two **6)** too.

Page 24 - Electricity
Good conductors - paperclip, needle, metal, drawing pin, wedding ring, nail.
Bad conductors - modelling clay, pencil, rubber, shell, wool, carrots.

Page 25 - Hidden treasure
1) mountains **2)** shipwreck **3)** fish **4)** ruins
5) dolphin **6)** tree.

Page 26 - Crossword
Across - 3 radio, 6 telephone, 8 thunder, 10 quiet, 12 hoot, 14 electricity, 17 woof, 18 ears.
Down - 1 candle, 2 torch, 4 straight, 5 instruments, 7 sun, 9 moo, 11 eyes, 13 miaow (or miaou), 15 two, 16 dark.

Page 27 - Speech marks
Richard - "Where are you?"
Samantha - "I am in the den."
Thomas - "What are you doing?"
Charlene - "We are having a picnic."

Page 28 - Beat the clock
1) 17 **2)** 10 **3)** 8 **4)** 5 **5)** 20 **6)** 38 **7)** 83
8) 15 **9)** 9 **10)** 7 **11)** 2 **12)** 7 **13)** 85 **14)** 2.

Page 29 - Alphabetical order
apple; **b**ear; **c**amel; **d**og; **e**lephant; **f**ish; **g**oat; **h**orse; **I**ndian; **j**igsaw; **k**angaroo; **l**ion; **m**onkey; **n**est; **o**ctopus; **p**eacock; **q**ueen; **r**abbit; **s**ock; **t**iger; **u**mbrella; **v**iolin; **w**hale; **x**ylophone; **y**o-yo; **z**ebra.

Page 30 - Favourite pets
1) 4 **2)** cat **3)** 29; 1st - cat; 2nd - rabbit; 3rd - hamster.

Page 30 - Index
1) 6-9; 52-53; 45; 65-68 **2)** buffalo **3)** animals.